DATE DUE

OCT 2 3 2006			

Demco, Inc. 38-293

THE GOLD RUSH

SALLY SENZELL ISAACS

Heinemann Library
Chicago, Illinois

© 2004 Heinemann Library
a division of Reed Elsevier Inc.
Chicago, Illinois

Customer Service 888-454-2279

Visit our website at www.heinemannlibrary.com

Produced for Heinemann Library by
   Bender Richardson White.
Editor: Lionel Bender
Designer and Page Makeup: Ben White
Picture Researcher: Cathy Stastny
Production Controller: Kim Richardson

07 06 05 04 03
10 9 8 7 6 5 4 3 2 1

Printed and bound by Lake Book Manufacturing, Inc.

Library of Congress Cataloging-in-Publication Data.
Isaacs, Sally Senzell, 1950-
   The Gold Rush / Sally Senzell Isaacs.
      p. cm.--(The American adventure)
   Includes bibliographical references (p.) and index.
   Contents: Sutter's Mill--Gold fever--Sacramento--Wagons heading west--Getting there by ship--San Francisco grows--The mining camps--Boomtowns--Digging deeper--Ghost town--California's future.
      ISBN 1-4034-2501-9 – ISBN 1-4034-4772-1 (pbk.)
   1. California--Gold discoveries--Juvenile literature.
   2. California--History--1846-1850--Juvenile literature.
   3. Frontier and pioneer life--California--Juvenile literature.
   [1. California--Gold discoveries. 2. California--History--1846-1850. 3. Frontier and pioneer life--California.]
   I. Title.
   F865.I83 2003
   979.4'04--dc21

                                          2003005589

Special thanks to Mike Carpenter and Geof Knight at Heinemann Library for editorial and design guidance and direction.

Acknowledgments
The producers and publishers are grateful to the following for permission to reproduce copyright material:
Californian Historical Society, page 17. Corbis Images/Phil Schermeister, page 25. Peter Newark's American Pictures, pages 7, 8, 10, 13, 14, 19, 20, 23. North Wind Pictures, page 26.

Illustrations by Nick Hewetson
Maps by Stefan Chabluk
Cover art by Nick Hewetson

QUOTATIONS

The quote on page 13 comes from *The Forty-Niners* by William Weber Johnson. New York: Time-Life Books 1974, page 61.

The quote on page 18 (Luzena Stanley Wilson) comes from *New Perspectives on the West* at website: www.pbs.org/weta/thewest/resources/archives/
   three/Luzena.html

The Author
Sally Senzell Isaacs is a professional writer and editor of nonfiction books for children. She graduated from Indiana University, earning a B.S. degree in Education with majors in American History and Sociology. She is the author of the nine titles in the *America in the Time of...* series published by Heinemann Library and of the first sixteen titles in Heinemann Library's *Picture the Past* series. Sally Senzell Isaacs lives in New Jersey with her husband and two children.

The Consultant
Our thanks to William E. Hill, historian, author of "Yesterday and Today" series of books on the Oregon, California, Santa Fe, and Mormon trails, for his assistance in the preparation of this book.

Note to the Reader
Some words are shown in bold, like **this**.
You can find out what they mean by looking in the glossary on page 30.

★★★★ ABOUT THIS BOOK

This book is about the California gold rush of 1848 to about 1854 and other events in America surrounding it. The term *America* means the United States of America (also called the U.S.) People heard about a discovery of gold in the hills near Sacramento, California, and thousands rushed there to try to get rich. Some people estimate that gold worth $250 million then (over $6 billion today) was dug up in California between 1848 and 1852. When it comes to specific numbers, we cannot always be sure what is true and what are just grand tales of overly excited miners. Historians seem to agree that the gold rush attracted more than 350,000 people to California in 12 years. These people came from all over the world, and many of them decided to stay and make California their home.

★★★★ CONTENTS

ABOUT THE SERIES

The American Adventure is a series of books about important events that shaped the United States of America. Each book focuses on one event. While learning about the event, the reader will also learn how the people and places of the time period influenced the nation's future. The little illustrations at the top left of each two-page article are a symbol of the times. They are identified in the Contents on page 3.

▼ This map shows the United States today, with the borders and names of all the states. Refer to this map, or to the one on pages 28 and 29, to locate places talked about in this book.

AMERICA'S STORY

Throughout the book, the yellow panels, showing an ocean-going passenger sailing ship, contain information that tells the more general history of the United States of America.

THE BOOK'S STORY

The green panels, showing a sack of gold nuggets, contain more detailed information about the California gold rush, this book's feature event.

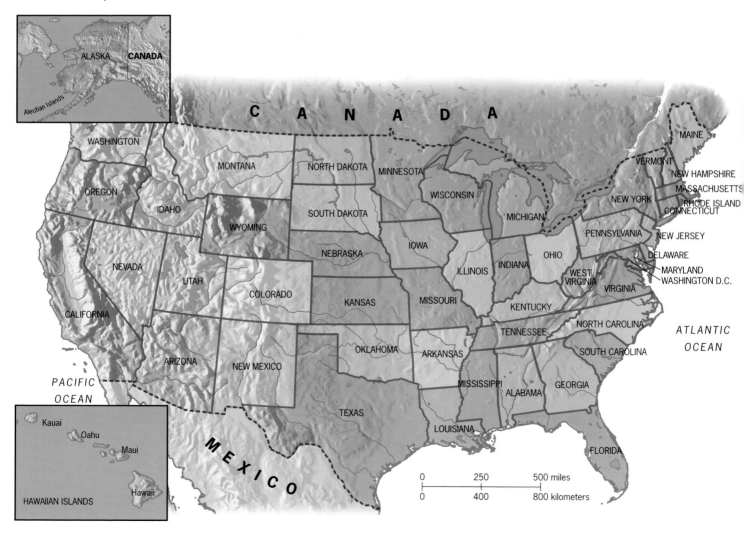

4

THE GOLD RUSH
INTRODUCTION

For thousands of years, pieces of gold washed down the mountains into the streams below California's Sierra Nevada. Long ago, about 300,000 American Indians lived in the area we call California. Whenever they fished in these streams, they probably saw this gold. But gold did not have the value to them that it had to the people who came later.

Gold had great value to the rulers of European countries, such as Spain. In the 1500s, Spain's rulers sent out explorers to search for gold in the New World, on land that we know as Peru, Mexico, and California. But it was not a Spanish explorer who found gold in California. It was an American construction worker named James Marshall on January 24, 1848.

Hundreds of thousands of people from around the world traveled to California. All of them dreamed of becoming rich. Many were disappointed. Still, in a few years, California changed from a sleepy wilderness to the 31st state in the nation. San Francisco, the coastal city closest to the gold mines, became the tenth largest city in the United States. The gold miners and the business owners who followed them made California the successful, energetic place it still is today. But their success wrecked the American Indians' way of life. In the end, most of them died in fights with the miners or from diseases that the miners carried. The land also suffered. As gold became scarce, miners used large machines to hack holes and tunnels into the mountains. Forests were destroyed and rivers became polluted.

There were many other gold rushes after this one, in such places as Colorado, Arizona, Alaska, Montana, Nevada and South Dakota. Still, many historians agree that the California gold rush was the most important in the nation's history.

SUTTER'S MILL

In 1839, few people talked about California. It was part of Mexico. Just a few thousand people lived there, mostly American Indians and Mexican families who owned ranches. There were some outsiders, U.S. citizens and Europeans, who moved to California to start a new life. John Sutter was one of them.

John Sutter had been a businessman in Switzerland. He loved to make and spend money. By 1834, he owed money to so many people that he decided to run away. He eventually landed in the Sacramento River valley of California. Sutter dreamed of starting a new **settlement** that would grow into a busy town. He thought people would be moving to California, and he would sell them food, clothing, and lumber to build their homes.

Sutter's new settlement grew. He started with a building surrounded with high walls for security. Later he added other buildings. The area became known as Sutter's Fort. Sutter hired American Indians to work for him, and they planted fruit trees and wheat fields. They also built a flour **mill** for turning wheat into flour. As Sutter had hoped, the fort attracted travelers and **settlers.** He soon decided he needed a sawmill to saw trees into lumber. Sutter hired a carpenter named James Marshall to choose a place for the **sawmill** and oversee the construction. Marshall found a site by the American River, about 50 miles (80 kilometers) from the fort in an area called Coloma. But Sutter did not own this land, and that would become a big problem later.

The discovery
On January 24, 1848, Marshall spotted a shiny metal in the muddy water. He picked it up and examined it. He thought it might be gold. In the pouring rain, Marshall rode his horse to Sutter's Fort to show the discovery to his boss. He demanded that Sutter lock the doors, then he uncovered his discovery. The two men performed several tests to find out what metal Marshall had found. The answer was "Gold!"

6

CALIFORNIA
1839 John Sutter arrives while California is still part of Mexico.
1846 In the Bear Flag **Revolt,** Americans in California take over Mexican offices in Sonoma, California. They declare California an independent **republic.**
1846 to 1848 The United States and Mexico fight the **Mexican War.**
1848 California becomes part of the United States.
1848 James Marshall discovers gold.
1850 California becomes the 31st state.

GOLD
$90,000

TO TELL IF IT IS GOLD
Marshall knew that gold could be beaten into a different shape without breaking. He also knew that strong chemicals could not change it. He did these tests:
• He hammered the metal with a rock. It flattened but did not break.
• He went to the camp's housekeeper, Jennie Wimmer, and asked her to drop the metal in the pot of **lye** she was boiling to wash clothes. After several hours, the gold was shiny as ever.

◀ This is Sutter's sawmill. Workers dug a channel to send water from the American River to the sawmill. The water turns a wheel that moves a blade. The blade cuts logs into boards.

▼ After many tests, Sutter (left) and Marshall knew there was gold in Coloma. Would the discovery make them rich? Or would hundreds of gold seekers rush to the land and ruin it?

7

GOLD FEVER

The workers on Sutter's sawmill dropped their tools and started looking for gold. Sutter panicked. He gathered his workers and promised to double their pay if they finished their work on the sawmill. He begged them to keep the gold discovery a secret.

▼ This is San Francisco around 1849. Sailors who traveled there for other reasons quickly heard about the gold. They left their ships and headed for the hills.

John Sutter's fields were growing and his stores were successful. He could not afford to have his employees stop working and start searching for gold. But the news was too huge to hide. Within six weeks of the discovery, nearly all his workers quit their jobs and headed for the gold fields. Some of them used bags of gold to pay for things in the stores at Sutter's Fort.

GOLD $90,000

SUTTER'S BAD LUCK

John Sutter did not own the land by his sawmill. He quickly tried to buy it from the American Indians who lived nearby. But the government of California said Indians had no rights to sell land. Thousands of miners started trampling through Sutter's fields, cutting through his fences, and setting his cattle free. They also shot the cattle for food.

The first millionaires

A man named Sam Brannan owned the **general store** at Sutter's Fort. He was also editor of a San Francisco newspaper called the *California Star*. Brannan found out about the gold and broke the news to San Francisco by marching through the streets with a bottle of gold dust and shouting, "Gold from the American River!"

Half the population of San Francisco, which was only about 850 people, rushed to Sutter's **sawmill**. And Brannan's store was ready for them. He had bought shovels, picks, pans, and blankets in San Francisco and sold them at outrageous prices at Sutter's Fort. For example, he bought pans at 20 cents each and sold them for as much as sixteen dollars. Brannan became one of California's first millionaires.

▲ These miners are shoveling dirt into a device called a rocker or cradle. They pour water over the dirt and rock the device. The dirt sifts out and washes away with water. The gold, if there is any, remains.

▶ Once the news hit San Francisco newspapers, hundreds of people ran to Sutter's sawmill. Photographers followed them to record the event.

SACRAMENTO

Many of the first people to reach the gold fields became very rich. In seven weeks, a man named Joe Dye made $40,000. That is nearly $1 million today. But soon gold became harder to find. The real millionaires were the store owners.

▼ Gold miners packed their belongings on their backs and headed for the gold fields.

The area around Sutter's Fort grew into the town of Sacramento. It was a bustling area with stores, hotels, and **saloons** where liquor was served and the entertainment was lively.

Throughout California, teachers, lawyers, blacksmiths, and farmers quit their jobs and headed for Sacramento. They bought a few tools and rode mules or horses into the hills of the Sierra Nevada where gold was supposed to be waiting for them. They set up tents or one-room cabins made of cartons. They learned about mining by watching those around them.

In November, the rainy season began, and the mines became very muddy. Many miners moved to Sacramento for the winter months. They stayed in **boardinghouses** where they paid for a bed and a hot meal each day. These miners needed food, clothes, medicine, and entertainment. Businesspeople hurried to Sacramento and opened stores and restaurants. Carpenters came to build new buildings.

Sutter's land

John Sutter held onto his fort and the land around it. But by 1849, he had huge bills to pay and no money coming in from his ruined fields. His son arrived from Switzerland to try to help him. John Sutter Jr. divided up the land and sold it. He managed to pay off most of his father's **debts.**

▶ On the Sacramento River, boats unload clothes, food, and supplies. These goods were sold in the stores along the busy main street. By December 1849, Sacramento had 30 businesses. These included a hotel, print shop, bakery, hospital, blacksmith shop, billiard room, barber shop, and bowling alley.

GOLD $90,000

SUTTER'S FORT

In 1849, John Sutter Jr. sold the fort, fields, houses, stores, and other buildings for $40,000. His father was relieved to get away from his debts and the strangers who ruined his land. By 1853, workers tore down the buildings to provide lumber for Sacramento. They took apart the flour **mill** and used the boards to build the City Hotel in Sacramento.

SACRAMENTO GROWS

In 1847, about 150 people lived in John Sutter's **settlement.** He called it New Helvetia, which was another name for New Switzerland. It later became part of Sacramento.

In 1850, California became a state in the United States, and Sacramento's population was 6,820. In 1854 Sacramento became the capital of California. By 1860, Sacramento's population was 13,785.

WAGONS HEADING WEST

About five years before gold fever hit, U.S. citizens had already caught Oregon fever. Thousands of families in the East put their possessions in wagons and walked from Missouri or Iowa to Oregon. They were willing to leave home for free land offered in the west.

When the news of the gold discovery spread, still more U.S. citizens moved west. These gold-seekers were different from the Oregon travelers. Most Oregon travelers were **emigrants.** They arrived with families to build new homes, farms, or businesses. But it was mostly men who traveled to California. They planned to live in the dirty mining camps, find gold, and return home as rich men.

THE MORMON TRAIL
Some forty-niners traveled on the Mormon Trail. This trail followed the Oregon Trail, then veered toward the Great Salt Lake in Utah. A few years earlier, Mormons, who were members of the Church of Jesus Christ of Latter-day Saints, started traveling this trail on their way to start a new community where they could practice their religion without criticism or attack. Their community became Salt Lake City. By 1853, about 10,000 people lived there.

12

► William Mount painted this picture of a post office in Long Island, New York. People dream of riches as they read a newspaper report from the gold mines. A poster on the wall advertises ships sailing from New York for California.

AFRICAN AMERICANS Some forty-niners from states in the South brought along their **slaves.** There were at least 1,000 African American slaves in the gold fields. About 1,000 free African Americans went to California on their own.

The wagon trains

In 1849, about 25,000 people traveled over land to California. The gold seekers began calling themselves forty-niners because of the year. Most traveled together in **wagon trains.** Some brought pack mules to carry their belongings. They walked through hot dusty deserts and over steep mountain cliffs. Sometimes American Indians, who feared they were losing their land, attacked the travelers.

People and animals suffered from sickness, starvation, and thirst. Some forty-niners came across a note that said, "Expect to find the worse desert you ever saw and then find it worse than you expected. Take water, be sure to take enough." Whenever travelers came to a stream or spring, they filled buckets, boots, coffee pots, and every other kind of container with water.

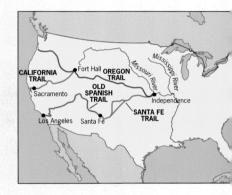

▲ California and Oregon travelers often started together on the Oregon Trail. Then, west of Fort Hall, in Idaho, gold seekers took the California Trail to Sacramento.

◄ Wagons got stuck in the rocks and deep sand of the hot Nevada desert. Travelers threw out clothing, tools, and even food to lighten their load. Animals died from lack of water and grass. People died from **cholera,** a disease that spread through unclean water.

13

GETTING THERE BY SHIP

People from midwestern states such as Missouri, Indiana, and Illinois took wagons to California. But people from New York, Boston, and other places along the Atlantic Ocean traveled by ship. There were two ways to reach California by water. They both brought unexpected adventure and problems.

Merchants' Express Line of Clipper Ships
FOR
SAN FRANCISCO!

NONE BUT A 1 FAST SAILING CLIPPERS LOADED IN THIS LINE.

THE EXTREME CLIPPER SHIP
OCEAN EXPRESS
WATSON, COMMANDER,
AT PIER **9**, EAST RIVER.

This splendid vessel is one of the fastest Clippers afloat, and a great favorite with all shippers. Her commander, Capt. WATSON, was formerly master of the celebrated Clipper "FLYING DRAGON," which made the passage in **97 days,** and of the ship POLYNESIA, which made the passage in **103 days.**

She comes to the berth one third loaded, and has very large engagements.

RANDOLPH M. COOLEY,
118 WATER ST., cor. Wall, Tontine Building.
Agents in San Francisco, DE WITT, KITTLE & Co.

Some ships left New York and sailed around the tip of South America and up the Pacific Ocean coast to San Francisco. Some of these ships were comfortable luxury ships, but many were whaling or cargo ships. Excited gold-seekers stayed crowded together in small rooms on wooden benches or shelves. The seas could get very rough, resulting in endless days of seasickness. It was impossible to keep food from rotting during the four to twelve month trip. To save time, some people took a ship to the **Isthmus of Panama** in Central America. Then they crossed the narrow piece of land by canoes and mules and took other ships that sailed up the Pacific coast.

▲ This 1851 poster advertises a trip from New York to San Francisco on a ship called the Ocean Express. Shipping companies promised the fastest trip to the gold mines. Then some got greedy and filled the ships with 300 passengers when there was only room for 100.

CROSSING PANAMA
Ships stopped on the Atlantic coast of the country of Panama. Passengers spent four days taking canoes and mules to the Pacific coast through jungles filled with mosquitoes and alligators. They slept in the jungle at night.

▶ After the long journey, people celebrated their first sight of San Francisco. Some owners of small boats paddled out to the ships to sell a ride to the shore. Others tried to buy or sell things. Many ships never left California again because their crews headed for the gold mines. Some ships were turned into hotels and stores.

14

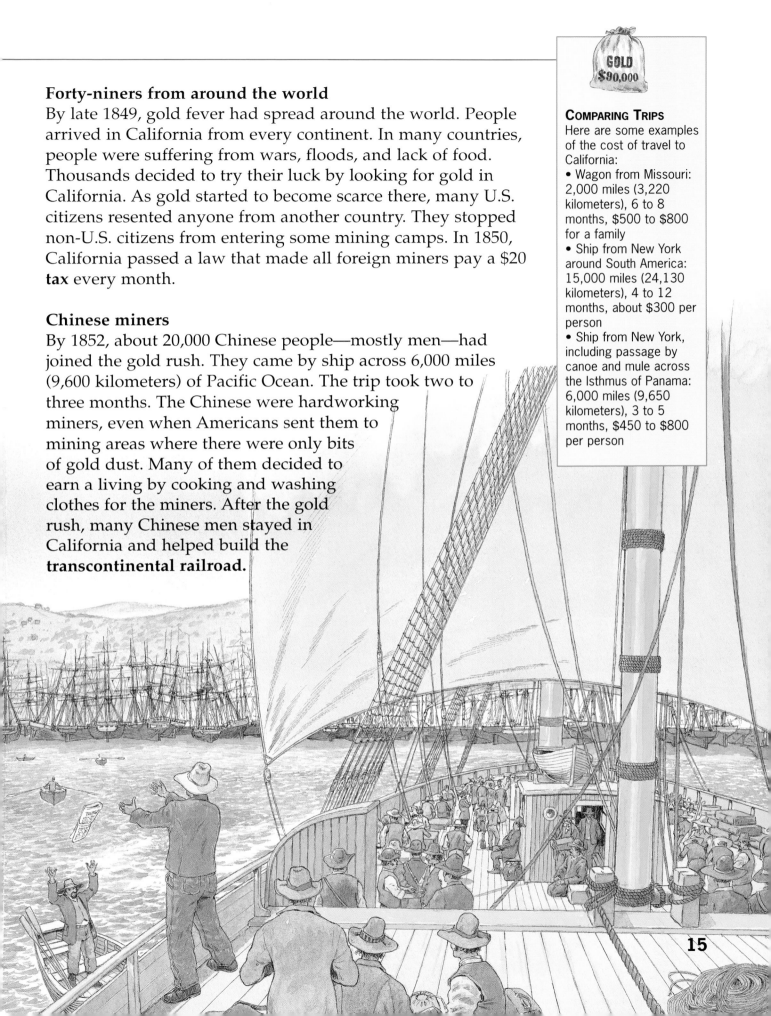

Forty-niners from around the world

By late 1849, gold fever had spread around the world. People arrived in California from every continent. In many countries, people were suffering from wars, floods, and lack of food. Thousands decided to try their luck by looking for gold in California. As gold started to become scarce there, many U.S. citizens resented anyone from another country. They stopped non-U.S. citizens from entering some mining camps. In 1850, California passed a law that made all foreign miners pay a $20 **tax** every month.

Chinese miners

By 1852, about 20,000 Chinese people—mostly men—had joined the gold rush. They came by ship across 6,000 miles (9,600 kilometers) of Pacific Ocean. The trip took two to three months. The Chinese were hardworking miners, even when Americans sent them to mining areas where there were only bits of gold dust. Many of them decided to earn a living by cooking and washing clothes for the miners. After the gold rush, many Chinese men stayed in California and helped build the **transcontinental railroad.**

GOLD $90,000

COMPARING TRIPS
Here are some examples of the cost of travel to California:
• Wagon from Missouri: 2,000 miles (3,220 kilometers), 6 to 8 months, $500 to $800 for a family
• Ship from New York around South America: 15,000 miles (24,130 kilometers), 4 to 12 months, about $300 per person
• Ship from New York, including passage by canoe and mule across the Isthmus of Panama: 6,000 miles (9,650 kilometers), 3 to 5 months, $450 to $800 per person

SAN FRANCISCO GROWS

San Francisco was once a sleepy little settlement. Just about 450 people lived there. But it happened to be located by the Pacific Ocean, with an excellent harbor. And it happened to be just 80 miles (128 kilometers) from Sutter's sawmill. When ships brought miners to California, most landed at the harbor in San Francisco.

THE FIRST JEANS
Levi Strauss had been a door-to-door salesman in New York City. During the gold rush, he sailed to San Francisco with rolls of heavy fabric. He thought he could sell the fabric to the miners for their tents. Then he got the idea to make sturdy pants with the fabric. The miners loved the pants, and "Levi's" have been popular ever since.

▼ A miner buys supplies in San Francisco before he heads out to dig for gold. **General stores** like this one sold everything from buttons to bullets. Sam Brannan's store brought in $36,000 in six weeks. That would be worth almost $830,000 today.

16

GOLD $90,000

By February 1850, more than 43,000 people had arrived in San Francisco by ship. Forty-niners stayed a few nights, and bought some clothes, food, and tools to take to the mining camp. San Francisco was also a town where lucky miners brought back their gold to spend on things they needed and to celebrate their good fortunes. Miners tossed down bags of gold to pay for liquor in the **saloons** and to gamble away on card games. Some miners used their gold to buy land in San Francisco or to open their own businesses. New restaurants, hotels, grocery stores, and other stores popped up almost overnight. These business owners made more money than the average miner in the gold fields.

Wild times

Some miners spent gold as if it would last forever. One miner called Flaxhead brought twenty pounds of gold dust into town. It was worth about $5,000 then and would be worth almost $115,000 now. He bought the most expensive meals and liquor, stayed in the best hotel's best room, and paid large gambling **debts.** Before returning to the mines, he bought some camping supplies and a boat ticket back up the Sacramento River to the mines. Then he poured the rest of the dust into a boot and carried it into a saloon. He kept buying drinks for everyone in the room until his boot was empty.

▲ S. F. Marryat painted this picture of San Francisco in 1851. Many of these buildings were shipped in pieces from the eastern United States and rebuilt in California.

Chinatown

People arrived in San Francisco from many different countries. When they arrived, they looked for others who spoke their language. They counted on friends or relatives who had arrived earlier to help them find places to live and work. Most of the 20,000 people who came to San Francisco from China moved to one neighborhood. The neighborhood became known as Chinatown. It looked like a little neighborhood from China in the middle of San Francisco.

THE MINING CAMPS

As soon as forty-niners arrived in California, they had one question: where is the gold? If a miner in town reported gold by a certain stream, the land around that stream quickly turned into a mining camp.

The mining camps had such names as Rich Flat, You Bet, and Poor Man's Creek. No one expected to stay long at a mining camp. Miners put up their tents and ran out to find a place to dig. A miner had to **claim** a piece of land before he dug. Each mining camp set up different claim laws. Some limited digging to an area as small as 10 square feet (3 square meters). Usually a miner could leave his tools at the site to show he claimed it. A miner could hold only one claim at a time. For that reason, some miners became partners. They agreed to share the gold from all their claims.

Bad luck or good luck?
Miners did not always follow the rules. A miner might try to "jump a claim," which means to sneak onto someone else's claim. Or he might sprinkle some gold flakes on his claim and then sell it for thousands of dollars. Nearly everyone heard stories about Thomas Stoddard. As one story goes, he claimed that he saw Gold Lake and promised to lead others there for a fee. Hundreds of miners followed him on a hopeless trip. Finally Stoddard ran off before the angry miners killed him. Three miners had a lucky break as they returned to camp. They found $36,000 worth of gold!

18

GOLD RUSH TERMS
Today we still use expressions that were first used during the gold rush.
• "Hit pay dirt" means find something good
• "Strike it rich" means make money quickly
• "Stake a claim" means say something belongs to you
• A "flash in the pan" is something that looks good but soon becomes disappointing

MEAL RUSH
Luzena Stanley Wilson moved to a mining camp with her husband and children. On their first day, Luzena bought two pieces of wood and set up a table. She bought some food and hung up a sign. She later wrote, "When my husband came back at night he found … twenty miners eating at my table. Each man as he rose put a dollar in my hand and said I might count him as a permanent customer."

▶ These miners have built a Long Tom—a water channel—to try to find gold among the dirt. They shovel in dirt, pour in water, and rock the Long Tom. Large rocks and heavier pieces of gold will not wash away. This mining camp is in the foothills of the Sierra Nevada. When the miners feel there is no more gold left, they will fold their tents and leave. Some will go to another camp. Others will go home.

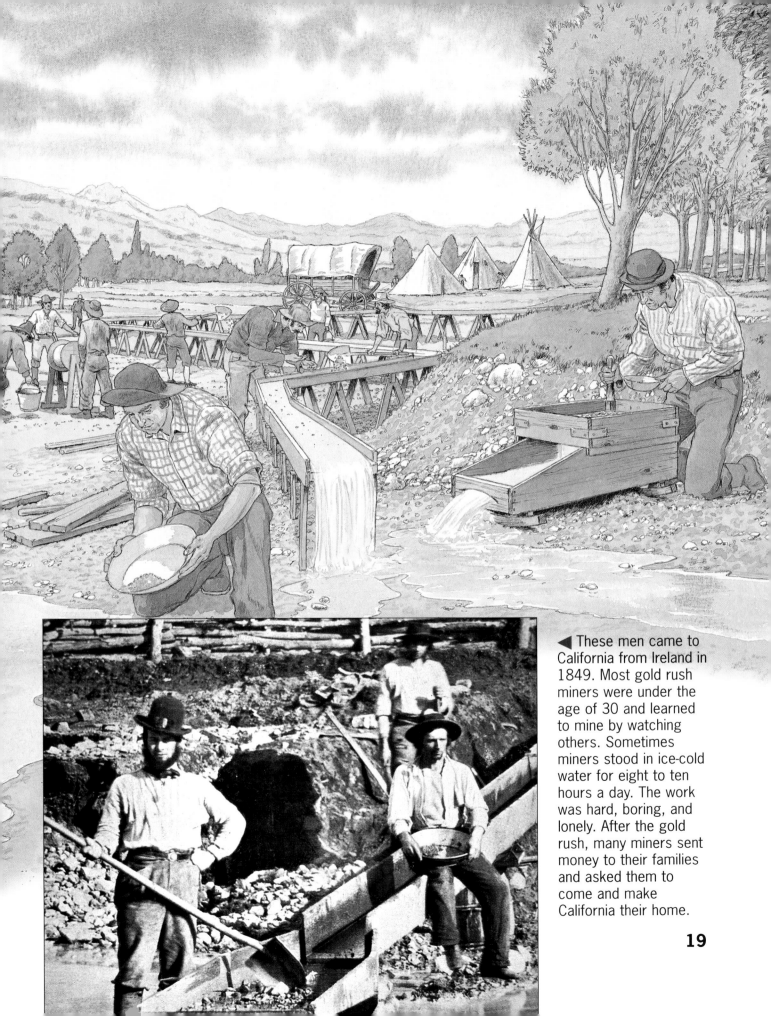

◄ These men came to California from Ireland in 1849. Most gold rush miners were under the age of 30 and learned to mine by watching others. Sometimes miners stood in ice-cold water for eight to ten hours a day. The work was hard, boring, and lonely. After the gold rush, many miners sent money to their families and asked them to come and make California their home.

19

BOOMTOWNS

Sometimes shabby mining camps grew into busy towns. The man who had started selling food from a wagon built a grocery store. The women who had served meals in her tent opened a hotel. Tents were replaced with cabins and houses. A town that grew out of a mining camp was called a boomtown.

The center of the town activity was usually the **general store.** While items were on sale in one part of the store, gambling tables were set up in another part. Upstairs there might have been a few bedrooms for rent. Miners came to the store to catch up on news, pick up their mail, and have some fun. Entertainers, with such names as Lotta Crabtree and Jeems Pipes, traveled among the mining towns with singing and comedy acts. At night, the store would be filled with drinking and singing by miners who were either celebrating their success or drowning their disappointment.

Miners with bad luck in the mines sometimes took out their anger on other miners. Some drank too much and fought too much. Many turned to robbery and murder. When this happened, the miners held their own quick trials. Sometimes 200 men formed a **jury** to decide on a punishment. A thief might be forced to leave the town. Punishments also included public whippings or even hangings.

STATEHOOD
In 1850, the U.S. had 15 states in the South that allowed slavery and 15 states in the North that did not. That year, California asked the U.S. Congress to let it to become a state. Because California was then slave-free, southern leaders said "No." After much arguing, Congress agreed to the **Compromise of 1850.** California became a free state, but other laws were passed that satisfied the South.

► Some women went to mining towns because they could choose a husband from hundreds of men. Others went to start businesses. They knew that California was one of the few places where a woman could make a living, and the money would belong to her, not to her husband or father.

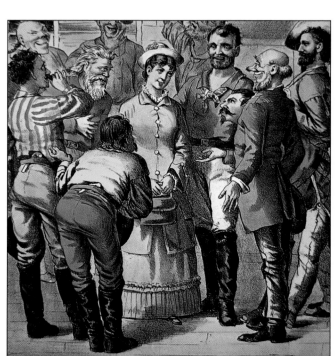

20

GOLD $90,000

SPANISH MINERS

Many forty-niners came from Mexico and South American countries, such as Chile. They often were expert miners because they had worked in mines back home. Some U.S. miners resented the Spanish-speaking miners, and sometimes physically attacked them. In 1850, a San Francisco newspaper, the *Evening Picayune*, reported that 30,000 to 40,000 miners from Chile and Mexico had already left California.

Wives needed

In the early gold rush days almost all the forty-niners were men. Soon some people decided that women could turn a wild town into something more proper. For example, Eliza Farnham sent a letter to newspapers in New York to encourage young women to come to California. Only three women agreed. However, in time, more women arrived, thanks to easier traveling by **stagecoaches** and a railroad across Panama. Many miners were eager to be married and to have someone cook and wash for them.

▼ By 1852, such towns as Downieville and Weaverville had hotels, doctors' offices, restaurants, barbers, drug stores, and tailors.

Here, a wagon train brings in food and supplies to stock the stores. In front, a wagon is carrying gold from the bank to a larger bank in San Francisco. Guards with guns ride alongside to protect the gold from robbers.

GROCERIE

21

DIGGING DEEPER

The first miners found gold easily. It was on the surface of the ground, mixed in with the dirt and rocks. By 1855, most of this gold was gone. Miners needed expensive machines to dig deeper. Some of them joined together to form mining companies.

Some miners found gold set into **quartz** rock that lay deep beneath the earth's surface. Quartz is a hard mineral that forms crystals. Mining companies bought big machines to crush the quartz into powder. Miners then washed the powdered rock in a way similar to the way they washed the **placer,** or surface, gold. This method did not produce much gold.

Tunnels

Some miners used shovels, picks, and drills to dig tunnels into hillsides. They tried to keep tunnels from collapsing by propping up wooden supports. The rocks from the tunnel produced a lot of gold. But the process was very dangerous. Sometimes tunnels caved in, and miners were buried alive.

Hydraulic mining

Another mining method was **hydraulic** mining. Miners took long, powerful hoses and blasted river water at a mountain or hillside. The water gouged huge holes in the land, washing down soil, rock, and—hopefully—gold. This method was terribly destructive. Tons of earth and trees were washed away. Sometimes they washed into valleys and ruined farmland.

22

GOLD VALUE
During the gold rush, an ounce of gold was usually worth $16. Here's what an ounce of gold has been worth at other times:
1934 $35
1973 $120
1980 $850
1993 $347
2003 $318

MAKING MONEY
In 1854, the United States opened a **mint** in San Francisco. A mint is a building where coins are made. Workers melted gold dust, poured it into strips, and punched out blank coins. Then workers used machines to stamp pictures and values on the coins. There were $20, $10, $5, $3, and $2.50 gold coins.

◀ On the edge of a mining town, buildings were set up to house machines that crushed rock, separated the gold, and removed the waste. The waste was piled up in mounds outside.

Townspeople worked for the mining company and lived in houses and huts close by.

▼ Miners, as well as business owners, brought their gold to banks:
• to exchange gold for coins and paper money
• to keep the gold or money safe
• to send money back home to their families.

This is a picture of a bank in Denver, Colorado, during its gold-mining days of the 1850s and 1860s. The clerk is weighing gold dust on a scale.

GHOST TOWNS

There is a saying that "Nothing lasts forever." That was true about the exciting times of the California gold rush. By 1855, most of the surface gold was gone, and with it the hope of thousands of miners.

When gold ran out, the miners listened for news of other discoveries. Many rushed off to Nevada, Colorado, Idaho, Canada, Alaska, and even Australia. Others packed up their cracked boots and faded shirts and went home. The gold rush was a disappointment to most of them. But they had a home to return to. The homeland of the American Indians was destroyed forever.

As the miners began to leave, there were fewer customers in the stores, **saloons,** and hotels. Whoever was left could not afford the high prices anymore. During the boom times, many businesses had taken loans from banks to buy more supplies. When the stores closed, the banks lost their loaned money and closed, too. Soon California was filled with **ghost towns,** buildings with no signs of life.

The silver rush

The gold rush ended in 1859, when silver was discovered near present-day Virginia City, Nevada. Henry Comstock took credit for spotting something "blue" in the rock he was mining. That "blue" turned out to be silver. News of this discovery reached the California mining towns, and miners rushed over the Sierra Nevada to get to the area that became known as the Comstock **Lode.** It turned out that the silver was too deep to dig out with shovels. Most of the miners went to work for large mining companies with expensive machines.

▼ These miners are packing up once again. Some are heading to new mines outside of California. Some are going home. Only a few lucky miners became rich. They had arrived soon after the 1848 discovery, and they dug up the richest mines. The rest of the gold was shared by tens of thousands of other miners. Had they stayed home, they probably would have earned more money at regular jobs.

J. STUDEBAKER
John M. Studebaker sold wheelbarrows to gold miners. When the gold rush ended, he took his $8,000 in profit and went home to Ohio. He started the Studebaker Wagon Corporation, making covered wagons for westward travelers. Years later, the company became a multi-million-dollar car maker.

▲ The town of Bodie, California, jumped to life in 1859 when William S. Bodey discovered gold there. It was known for its 65 **saloons,** street fights, and robberies. When the gold ran out, so did the people. Bodie became an empty ghost town.

AFRICAN AMERICANS
From 1850 to 1858, California lawmakers tried to pass a **bill** to keep African Americans from entering the state. Those who already lived there would not be allowed to bring in their families. In April 1858, it seemed as if the bill would pass. So approximately 900 African Americans moved to Victoria, Canada. Though the bill never passed, California lost one-fifth of its black population.

GOLD $90,000

CALIFORNIA'S FUTURE

The gold rush lasted less than ten years. By the time it ended, California had changed forever. It had cities and towns and settlers from every continent. Even without the gold, people still wanted to make California their home.

Before James Marshall discovered gold in 1848, California was a little-known land where some American Indians, Spanish Californians, and other **settlers** lived. Then the gold rush turned California into a household name. All over the world, people talked about friends or relatives who traveled to "Gold Mountain." Books and newspapers were filled with gold rush stories. Even though the rush for gold died down by 1855, California still seemed like a "land of golden opportunity." By 1860, there were 380,000 people living in the state.

Staying in California
California had a mild climate and rich soil for farming. Many former miners and newcomers started farms and ranches. The demand for beef and farm products grew with the population. Doctors, lawyers, judges, and teachers found plenty of opportunities for work in California's towns and cities. Workers also were needed to construct buildings, homes, and railroads. To provide services to the newcomers, people started businesses of all types: shoe stores, broom factories, and butcher shops.

▶ This is a picture of Chinatown in 1880. By then the neighborhood took up 12 blocks of San Francisco. The air was filled with the sound of spoken Chinese. The people in the lower left corner are doing laundry. At that time, many U.S. citizens favored laws to keep the Chinese out of the United States.

From coast to coast

As California grew, all U.S. citizens began to look at their nation differently. The people of the United States were no longer clustered in eastern cities with a few farms through the Midwest. The nation—and its people—truly stretched from coast to coast.

JOHN SUTTER

Although the gold rush started on his land, John Sutter had no luck finding gold. The flood of miners in 1848 ruined his land, which he eventually sold to pay his **debts.** Sutter lived on a nearby farm until fire destroyed his house in 1866. He then left California and moved to Lititz, Pennsylvania. Sutter died in 1880 at the age of 77. Today, Sutter's Fort State Historic Park in Sacramento helps tell us about the gold rush.

JAMES MARSHALL

James Marshall may have found the first nugget of gold, but he still died a poor man.

Once the news of gold spread, other miners forced him off the land. He had no luck at other mines either. He drifted from place to place and eventually settled in Kelsey, California, where he worked as a blacksmith. He died in 1885 at the age of 75. He is buried on a hilltop that now overlooks Marshall Gold Discovery Park in Coloma.

◀ San Francisco became one of the nation's most famous cities. Banks, other businesses, and shipping companies that started in the gold rush grew larger in the following years.

In the 1850s, the city had 15 firehouses, 16 hotels, 12 daily newspapers, 3 hospitals, and 537 **saloons.** Ships steamed in every day, bringing goods and people from all over the world. In 1869, the first railroad from the eastern United States reached San Francisco. Wagons and **stagecoaches** clattered along the dirt streets. This picture shows a neighborhood called Nob Hill. Wealthy citizens lived in these mansions.

HISTORICAL MAP OF THE UNITED STATES

ALASKA
CANADA
Aleutian Islands

This is the United States in 1850. Nearly the entire mainland of the nation was complete. Only a tiny strip called the Gadsen Purchase was bought from Mexico in 1853. In 1850, California became the 31st state. Thousands of people were crossing the country to get to Oregon and California. From 1869, the transcontinental railroad would make the trip faster and easier.

WASHINGTON

Columbia River

OREGON CESSION 1846

OREGON

MONTANA

Missouri River

IDAHO

Snake River

Fort Hall

WYOMING

Sacramento River

American River

Promontory Point

Ogden

NEVADA

Salt Lake City

UTAH

Sacramento
Sutter's Fort
Sutter's Mill

San Francisco

MEXICAN CESSION 1848

COLORADO

Ship route from New York to San Francisco via the Panama Canal

SIERRA NEVADA MOUNTAINS

CALIFORNIA

ARIZONA

Los Angeles

Colorado River

Gila River

Salt River

Santa Fe

NEW MEXICO

--- River

·ııııııı· Transcontinental Railroad

······· Oregon Trail

······· California Trail

······· Santa Fe Trail

······· Old Spanish Trail

······· Butterfield Overland Mail

⬭ Silver

⬭ Gold

⬭ Gold and Silver

GADSDEN PURCHASE 1853

El Paso

MEXICO

PACIFIC OCEAN

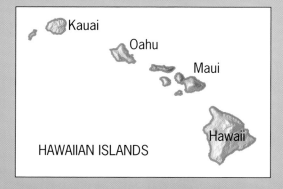

Kauai

Oahu

Maui

Hawaii

HAWAIIAN ISLANDS

| 0 | 250 | 500 miles |
| 0 | 400 | 800 kilometers |

Hudson Bay

CANADA

NORTH DAKOTA

MINNESOTA

Lake Superior

Missouri River

SOUTH DAKOTA

WISCONSIN

Lake Huron

MICHIGAN

Lake Michigan

Mississippi River

St. Lawrence

MAINE

Lake Champlain

VERMONT

NEW HAMPSHIRE

Lake Ontario

NEW YORK

MASSACHUSETTS

Boston

RHODE ISLAND

CONNECTICUT

Lake Erie

Hudson River

NEBRASKA

IOWA

Chicago

ILLINOIS

INDIANA

OHIO

Pittsburgh

PENNSYLVANIA

Delaware River

New York City

NEW JERSEY

Philadelphia

DELAWARE

MARYLAND

Washington, D.C.

Omaha

Independence

St. Louis

MISSOURI

KANSAS

Ohio River

KENTUCKY

WEST VIRGINIA

VIRGINIA

Richmond

ATLANTIC OCEAN

OKLAHOMA

ARKANSAS

TENNESSEE

NORTH CAROLINA

Mississippi River

Memphis

SOUTH CAROLINA

Atlanta

Charleston

GEORGIA

Savannah

TEXAS

MISSISSIPPI

ALABAMA

LOUISIANA

ATLANTIC OCEAN

New Orleans

FLORIDA

Rio Grande River

Ship route from New York to San Francisco via the Panama Canal

GULF OF MEXICO

CUBA

CARIBBEAN SEA

29

GLOSSARY

bill written plan for a new law, to be discussed in Congress

boardinghouse house where meals and a sleeping room are provided for pay

cholera disease in the stomach and intestines that causes vomiting and diarrhea. It is spread by unclean water.

claim to say that an area of land belongs to you. The land is also called a claim.

Congress part of the United States government in which representatives make laws

debt money that is owed to another person

emigrant person who leave his or her home to move to a new area or country

general store place that sells many different things, such as food, clothing, and tools

ghost town deserted town

hydraulic mining method of mining in which powerful jets of water were blasted to loosen gold from the rocks and hillsides

Isthmus of Panama narrow strip of land that connects the Atlantic and Pacific Oceans and connects North and South America.

jury group of people who decide whether a person is guilty or innocent

lode crack in rock that has metal in it

lye harsh liquid used to make soap and clean clothes

Mexican War (1846 to 1848) war fought between the United States and Mexico. In the end, the United States acquired California, Nevada, and Utah, most of Arizona and New Mexico, and parts of Wyoming and Colorado.

mill building with machines for grinding grain to make flour

mint place where coins are made

placer sand, gravel, or earth in the bed of a stream that contains particles of gold or other valuable minerals

quartz hard mineral that forms crystal

republic place where people elect representatives to manage their country

revolt rise against the government or authority

saloon place where alcoholic drinks are sold

sawmill building with machines that saw wood into lumber

settlement group of buildings, and the people living in them

settlers people who make a home in a new place

slave person who is owned by another person and is usually made to work for that person

stagecoach boxlike car pulled by horses in which people traveled long distances

tax money paid to a government that is used to run a town, state, or country

transcontinental railroad train tracks going across a continent

wagon train group of covered wagons that traveled to the West together

TIMELINE OF EVENTS IN THIS BOOK

1839 John Sutter arrives in California

1841 The first organized **wagon trains** head for Oregon and California

1846 to 1848 The United States and Mexico fight the **Mexican War,** and California becomes part of the United States in 1848

1848 James Marshall discovers gold at John Sutter's sawmill near present-day Sacramento

1848 to 1854 Nearly 500,000 people arrive in California during the main years of the California gold rush

1848 to 1854 Nearly 50,000 American Indians die in California, mainly due to the crowd of miners who arrive

1849 John Sutter's land is sold as Sacramento grows into a busy city

1850 California becomes the 31st state

1854 Sacramento becomes the capital of California

1856 The first overland mail service to California begins with the mail traveling by **stagecoach**

1858 About 900 African Americans leave California for Victoria, Canada, fearing a law that would try to keep African Americans from entering California

1859 Silver is discovered in an area called the Comstock Lode in Nevada, causing a rush to Nevada and ending the California gold rush

1869 Transcontinental railroad connects California with the eastern United States

BOOKS TO READ

Blumberg, Rhoda. *The Great American Gold Rush.* New York: Bradbury Press, 1989.

Ito, Tom. *The California Gold Rush.* San Diego: Lucent Books, 1997.

Stanley, Jerry. *Hurry Freedom – African Americans in the Gold Rush.* California. New York: Crown Publishers, 2000.

PLACES TO VISIT

Bodie State Historic Park
P.O. Box 515
Bridgeport, CA 93517
Telephone: (760) 647-6445

Marshall Gold Discovery Park
310 Back Street
Coloma, CA 95613
Telephone: (530) 622-347

Sutter's Fort State Historic Park
2701 L Street
Sacramento, CA 95816
Telephone: (916) 445-4422

INDEX